Creating Your DREAM Retirement

How to Live Your DREAM and Leave a Legacy

Bev Bertram

Michelle Bertram

CONTENTS

Introduction

"Do we have enough to retire?" asked the Petersons, a hard-working Midwest couple with a very healthy portfolio. They had come to our office wanting a second opinion. Having already asked this same question of their advisor, they were not satisfied with the ho-hum answer they received.

The question is a common one, intertwined with other queries: Will we have enough income during retirement? What if the market crashes again—will we still be okay? Will we be able to travel as we always planned? Is Uncle Sam going to benefit from our hard work more than we will? Will we have any legacy to pass to our children and grandchildren?

All these inquiries boil down to a single question: "Will I be able to live my DREAM Retirement?"

People ask that question in different ways because everyone's DREAM retirement is a little different. But the heart of the matter is identical. People are looking for peace of mind, security, and financial freedom to be able to enjoy their golden years.

This book and the DREAM Retirement Process is dedicated to answering that one question. When you have a DREAM retirement plan in place and can confidently answer YES, you will experience peace of mind, security, and financial freedom in unprecedented ways. You will truly be able to live your DREAM and leave a legacy!

PART I.
THE BIRTH OF THE DREAM

1. A Story

The story of the DREAM Retirement Process begins a few decades ago with the birth of a thirteenth child....

Bev Bertram's Story

My story starts off at high speed. When I was born, my mom and dad already had a dozen kids running around the house. There were five boys and seven girls, and the eighth girl made thirteen. And when I was born, Mom and Dad divorced. Dad had a problem with alcohol and we didn't see him after that.

As you can imagine, Mom worked hard and struggled to support us and raise us. I saw how hard she worked for so long, and from a young age, I learned a couple things. Two things in particular have stuck with me and become a driving force in my whole life.

First, I saw how important hard work is. You just have to do it. Sometimes you don't think you can do it, but you do it and you survive. You have to do the hard work to keep your commitments and to take care of your responsibilities, and if you keep it up, you make it.

Another thing that made a substantial impression on me was the reality that life is very hard when you're struggling financially. When there's no provision or guidance and you have to make it all happen yourself, that's hard.

As you might also guess, because my family was so large and Dad wasn't there, it wasn't easy for me to fit in.

You probably know that at school there are a couple different crowds. There are the jocks (the athletes) and the brains (the studious ones). You also know there is the **in** crowd—the popular kids, the ones everyone wants to be like and hang around. And there is the **definitely not in** crowd, the leftover kids who were loners or who dressed funny or who came from different situations that nobody else did.

Of course, I was part of the **not in** crowd. Not only did I stick out because I was always dressed in hand-me-downs, but I was also shy. I struggled with that. The only group I fit into was the **not in** crowd.

I was sensitive to anyone who was pushed into the **not in** crowd. One thing that burned me up was when one of us got picked on for no reason. That happened all the time, of course, because the **in** crowd always needed someone to torment.

To this day, I remember an incident with my friend, Cindy, who was in the **not in** crowd with me. I recall vividly being in the stairwell with her when she was being picked on for no good reason. I thought "This is not right." I didn't think there was anything right about it when they were picking on me, but it lit a fire in me when they were picking on someone else. So I stood up for Cindy. I told the girls to back off and leave her alone. Of course, I immediately got pushed down the stairs and got bruised up.

I didn't realize the impact that day, but it's that passion that has carried me forward to this day. I got into financial services with a passion to help people when they're struggling to get the pieces together, struggling with missing pieces, or trying to make it happen without good advice or a good example.

One of the first things I realized is that the financial services world is full of bullies. There are financial companies and brokers and advisors out there who trying to cram products and services down the throats of unsuspecting folks who are trying to get it right with their money. They're pounding square pegs into round holes. Then there is the financial media that is full of misinformation, and that aggravates me to no end.

I've watched people I know get bad advice and get taken advantage of by financial professionals with a sales quota agenda, and I remember my friend Cindy in the stairwell, and it burns me up.

I have a passion to make sure that people don't miss out on opportunities. If they've been blessed with financial resources, I need to see that they don't miss their best opportunities due to bad information or misguided advisors who are trying to make their client's situation fit into products and services that are simply not appropriate. And that's why I do what I do—why we created the DREAM Retirement Process.

MICHELLE BERTRAM'S STORY

One day at age eight I sat in the living room and talked with my mom, who was cleaning curtains near the wall and entryway. I asked her, "Why does everyone leave us?" My grandma had just died unexpectedly. My cousins—the ones I played with all the time—had just moved away. And my dad was gone all week for his trucking job.

I knew it was hard on my mom too. She started sleepwalking again (after a sleepwalking-free period) and even locked herself outside in the middle of the night. She does not remember this, but I do. I remember her calling my name in the middle of the night: "Michelle, come open the door!"

Loved ones' absence dragged both me and my mom down. I felt hurt and alone. But it was time for me to step up. As the oldest, I became the third "adult" in the house. My mom needed me. My sisters needed me.

My caretaking instincts manifested themselves from an early age. When I was five years old, I had three younger siblings. Four kids under six years old is enough to drive anyone crazy! One morning near breakfast my mom had to step out of the room to clear her head. All my little sisters were crying, and I remember putting the baby in the swing and telling the others, "Everything will be okay." Protecting and caretaking is in my blood. I showed it at five, and I showed it at eight.

Fast forward to age 20. I joined my mom, Bev, in business—pretty much because I wanted to be able to do Missions work and have a flexible work schedule. It seemed like a good job that would provide a solid income and give me the flexibility to make a difference with Missions work outside the country. I didn't know that much about the industry when I started, just that Mom liked it. She'd been able to be there for us as we'd grown up and that sounded good to me.

I was young and naïve, like most 20 year olds, in my approach to this new adventure. I thought it would be easy and that I knew it all. And I can remember when I was first hit with some of the reality of the financial services industry, some of the ways it works.

Mom and I were sitting at a kitchen table with the Whites, a couple who had requested her to come help them plan their estate. This was early in my training, about 2001 or 2002. The TV was on with stock market news and the Whites were only half tuned into us. They were more tuned into watching the stock market. In talking with them, we found out that they had all their hard-earned retirement money at risk in the market. Nothing was in protected accounts; there was no principal safety or guarantees.

Now the Whites were about as conservative as they come. They hated the risk. They told us they couldn't sleep at night because they were worried about their investments and we could see the stress in their eyes. The weight of their worry was evident in their appearance. They had brought us there to talk about estate planning—but they were too worried about their current investment situation to think beyond the moment.

When we left, I remember thinking "And these are supposed to be the Golden Years? What is the point to work hard and save just to spend your retirement worried about whether the market is up or down? There has to be a better way!"

We worked out a plan with them to address the amount of risk they were taking in their investments. The goal was to re-allocate their investments to provide more principal protection and reduce the amount of market risk they were taking so they could sleep at night. This was the first step in any estate planning work: if we didn't take care of the risk, their biggest worry, we knew they would not be able to even think about setting up any type of estate plan. They would not be able to mentally handle it.

We started a meeting by reviewing the plan with them. When we explained how it would lessen the amount of market risk and provide them with some much-desired principal protection and guarantees, we could see the relief wash over their faces.

This is when another industry reality hit me again.

The first step to implementing this plan was for them to call their current custodian to make a sale of some of their investments and move to cash to stop the bleeding. The custodian, however, called their broker to tell him what the clients were doing and the broker called the clients. He basically told them they couldn't or should do anything, that they just needed to wait and everything would be fine. It didn't matter how much they told him about how they felt about it. He just blew them off and totally disregarded their feelings. He acted like the money was his, not theirs.

He intimidated them to the point where they froze. They wanted to make a change, but they did not have the energy to fight with their broker, so they gave in.

That was the last we saw of the Whites. I thought of them often over the next couple years, especially when the next bear market happened. I wondered how they were doing and wished we could have helped them.

The whole experience made me angry at our industry. I found that the only thing most advisors cared about was pushing their products, not planning with their clients. They seemed to be more interested in padding their pockets at the expense of their clients. Wall Street and their brokers are not at all connected with the concerns of Main Street Americans. Clients are treated more as commodity, without thought of their dreams and hopes. There is no personal appreciation for the hard work that was put into accumulating that wealth, nor the children and charities dear to the client's heart.

I vowed then to make a difference. I knew we could not transform the industry, but at least we would not be conformed to the industry. Our goal was then, and is now even more, to help ensure that the Golden Years are truly golden.

I had thought I could use a career in financial planning to keep space in my life for other difference-making work. I've since realized that my career itself had a bigger purpose. It changed from being a job to a purpose—to make a real difference for our clients.

2. Which One of These Is Not Like the Others?

Sesame Street is a classic. Michelle watched it as a kid, and now her boys watch it. We bet you have watched it too. One part of the show forever sticks in my head. They show four pictures on the screen—all similar, but one slightly different. Then begins the song: "Which one of these is not like the others?"

Our client Joe reminded us of that song a few months ago. He was searching for an advisor he felt comfortable with. After attending various financial seminars and meeting multiple advisors, he visited our office for a retirement conversation. He asked a simple question: "What makes you different from other advisors?"

To Joe—and to so many others—all financial advisors look relatively the same. As do the pictures on Sesame Street. And in some respects, what we do at Bertram Financial isn't all that different from most other financial services companies. We serve individuals and families looking forward to retirement with retirement income planning, estate and legacy planning. We work closely with companies to provide company retirement plans. We also serve business owners to provide advanced tax planning, tax reduction and cost savings.

At the same time, we are quite different from our financial advisor colleagues. Because we are independent advisors, we have the ability to partner with the best professionals and access the best financial tools and products in the industry. We aren't restricted and controlled by a parent company with a limited range of options.

We are proud to be able to offer Red, Yellow and Green Money solutions *(See Chapter 11)* for our clients, in contrast to most advisors. It's important for us to be able to tailor income plans for very specific client goals with principal-protected Green Money as well as Red Money that will continue to ensure growth while reducing risk. Many advisors are not able to utilize both types of money, for a variety of reasons. However, we feel it is essential to be able to place money in each kind of account for different purposes toward the same retirement. Limited placement options can be crippling to wealth.

We are strongly committed to macro financial planning and a team approach. A macro approach looks at all areas of a financial plan: investment and income goals, tax and estate planning, as well as risk management and insurance coverage. To provide a macro financial plan, we work with other professionals—such as CPAs, attorneys, money managers, and other financial advisors—to create and execute the optimal retirement plan for our clients' unique needs and goals. A great number of our colleagues focus only on the aspects of their clients' business that falls within the scope of products and services that they are authorized and trained to deal with. Other concepts are not even mentioned.

FAMILY BUSINESS, FAMILY VALUES

As a family business, we bring family values into our client relationships.

The first relationship we value is our relationship with God. We strive to honor Him in all we do. We practice financial stewardship that would be pleasing to Him.

As financial advisors, we invest in our relationships with our clients, seeking to understand their needs, goals and desires as we develop a financial plan for them. We are deeply rooted in the concept of excellence and personal service in the financial planning process. We believe in open and honest communication, creating a family environment and having fun with people who are likable, coachable and ethical.

We also value coaching—growth and learning— both for our clients and for ourselves. As financial advisors, we add to our knowledge by attending multiple coaching and professional training events each year. We believe in a humble attitude, an open mind, a commitment to act and passion for a purpose. We know that coaching helps us all grow and make the impact we want to make.

As mentioned in our personal stories, we are both on a mission to change our industry, stand up to financial bullies and help people live their dreams. This is why we created the DREAM Retirement Process. Following this process, we help you create and secure your DREAM Retirement.

Upon hearing this, Joe knew he had found the financial advisor "not like the others." The Sesame Street friends would be proud.

3. Dreaming from Start to Finish

The DREAM Retirement Process Overview

> ALL MEN DREAM, BUT NOT EQUALLY. THOSE WHO DREAM BY NIGHT IN THE DUSTY RECESSES OF THEIR MINDS, WAKE IN THE DAY TO FIND THAT IT WAS VANITY: BUT THE DREAMERS OF THE DAY ARE DANGEROUS MEN, FOR THEY MAY ACT ON THEIR DREAMS WITH OPEN EYES, TO MAKE THEM POSSIBLE.
>
> – T. E. LAWRENCE "OF ARABIA"
> AUTHOR, STATESMAN, SOLDIER

Whether you run your own business or are employed by a company, ultimately we are all working towards the same thing—our DREAM Retirement.

Here are four pillars of a DREAM retirement:

- Becoming the person you want to be
- Doing the things you want to do (when you want to do them)

- Being with the people you want to be with
- Having the impact you want to have (making the difference you want to make)

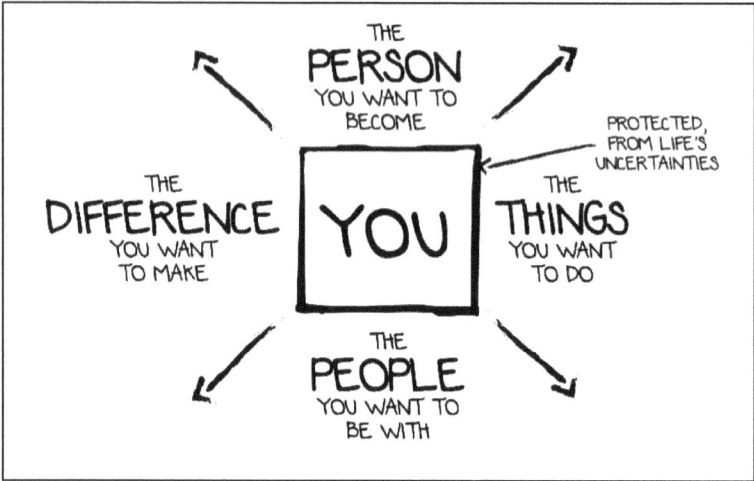

Imagine you have embarked on a journey to become the person you want to be. As you walk along that road, you are doing all the things you always wanted to do. Beside you are the people you love. And as you travel, you are making a difference in the lives of all those you meet. This journey is a picture of the DREAM Retirement.

In the illustration above, you are in the middle surrounded by a box. Why? The four pillars of a DREAM Retirement are essential, but one more thing must be added: protection against life's uncertainties.

Back in ancient times, a land's rulers protected their valuables by building a wall and a moat. You are the ruler of your DREAM Retirement, and the principle still stands today. You need to protect yourself from life's uncertainties.

The DREAM Retirement Process builds a wall and a moat around your DREAM Retirement. With them in place, you will have increased control, peace, freedom, and impact potential.

"I know I need a retirement plan, but where should I start?" asked the Smiths, a retiring professional couple.

That's a very good question, one we have heard quite often over the years in our work with retirees and those planning to retire. That is why we created the DREAM Retirement Process.

Many people think of retirement planning just in terms of numbers: How much do I need to have saved for retirement? How much income do I need to generate in retirement? But we believe a DREAM Retirement is about more than just numbers.

We look at retirement as *Becoming who you want to be, doing the things you want to do, spending time with those you want to spend time with, and having the impact you want to have, all while being protected from life's uncertainties.* Our DREAM Retirement Process is a four-step process based on that foundation.

1. Paint Your DREAM Picture

As the first step in the DREAM Retirement Process, we ask you to "Paint a Rockwell" of your future. What do you want to do? Who do you want to be with? What would a great retirement look like to you? A real clear picture is the starting point for a good plan.

2. Identify Obstacles—Seen and Unseen

"Some of these obstacles are easy to see," said Mr. Wilson, a retiring business owner, "but how do I identify obstacles that are unseen?" That is a million-dollar question. The fact is, most retirees and pre-retirees are not aware of some of the obstacles they will face in retirement. Therefore, it is important to walk through these steps with a professional advisor who works with people just like you every day. They have firsthand knowledge of what obstacles their clients face. You can learn from other people's experiences and identify obstacles before they become problematic.

3. Create Your DREAM Blueprint

If you had 100 people design their dream house, chances are you would end up with 100 different blueprints. We are all a little different. The right solution for one person is not right for another. For this reason, it is important to design a DREAM Retirement blueprint that is unique to you—just as your dream home would not come from a prefab design. If you want to create a DREAM Retirement, you can't use a cookie cutter financial plan.

4. Outline Actions to Take

> "Vision without action is merely a dream. Action without vision just passes the time. Vision with action can change the world"
> Joel A. Barker

For your Retirement DREAM to become a reality, you must act. The key is knowing how to act. To do something just to do something is action without vision. That is why the action steps are the last step of the process: We first need to determine our direction, obstacles, and plan. Only then can we act. Skipping any of the previous steps leads to passing time but going nowhere. And on the flip side, completing the first three steps but failing to take action ensures your DREAM Retirement will stay just that—a dream.

These four steps are the pathway to creating a DREAM Retirement...to becoming who you want to be, doing what you want to do, spending your time with whom you want to be with, and making the impact you want to make!

We created the DREAM Retirement Process to enable you to live your DREAM Retirement. We will stand up for you.

PART II.
THE DREAM RETIREMENT PROCESS

4. What You Want – Paint Your Dream Retirement Picture

Several years ago our family took a trip to Hawaii. The whole trip started because of a conversation with my Grandma Joyce, who told us she always wanted to go to Hawaii. Coming from Joyce, this surprised us. See, Joyce has never traveled. She leads a quiet, scheduled life. Every day she rises at ten to seven. Sleeping late is five to seven, and awakening early is quarter to seven. She eats at the same time each day; she goes shopping the same day each week. Everything about her is scheduled.

Hawaii? Really? She explained: she wanted to take her shoes off and walk on a sandy beach looking out over the water of the Pacific Ocean. She vividly remembers the day Japan attached Pearl Harbor, the devastation and loss that all Americans felt, and the hard years during the war. But through it all she remembered the courage of our nation, the determination to win, and the overcoming feeling of triumph when the war was done. She wanted to go to Pearl Harbor, relive it all, and honor those who fought for all of us.

Grandma Joyce had a vision behind her Hawaii dream. Likewise, a lot of vision lies behind retiring. We want to paint your DREAM Retirement lifestyle the same way Joyce painted her dream vacation.

Many times, retirement is thought of only in terms of numbers—the financial information, the money in the bank and how long it will last at what sort of level. Many financial planners focus on the money, but they don't stop to ask you want you are trying to fund.

The truth is that wealth also involves a social and personal dimension, not just the financial. Yes, you have the money, but it's the money that supports the activities you want to do. The money allows you to be with the people you want to be with and be a part of the community issues and programs you want to influence and support.

Have you spent any time thinking about what you want your retirement to look like? In practical terms? At the very end, what will you want to look back on and be satisfied with?

What about wealth is important to you? The answers to this question are the social and emotional dimensions of retirement wealth.

When you make decisions about your wealth, you're making changes because of the things you want to do and the people you want to spend time with. The dollars and cents matter because of your social and personal goals.

If you don't know what you are trying to fund, how will you know if you have enough? Will your financial planner be able to tell the truth when you ask if you can retire at 65 and get that RV and winter in Arizona and send all six grandkids to college? Will he even know?

So again, what do you want your retirement to look like?

There are two major components to consider when you're sketching out your DREAM Retirement, two pillars of wealth. Let's look at lifestyle and legacy.

LIFESTYLE – DREAMS

The lifestyle of your retirement is going to be fairly obvious to you. You have a good idea as to whether you want to travel and spend a couple months of every year with each of the kids. Maybe you've been dreaming of when you can stay home and build furniture in the basement and get more active at church. Maybe you're yearning to sell the house, buy a cabin in the Pacific Northwest and spend your days fishing and making quilts with your lifetime friends. Do you have prize-winning roses to raise and show? Maybe it's time to throw yourself into political or social activism.

Draw a mental picture of the life you want to live in retirement. Get out your notepad and pencil and write a few things down. This is the first part of the

DREAM Retirement Process that we will lead you through.

We frequently get asked "How much do I need to retire?" This question can't be answered right off the cuff. There's no one right answer that applies to more than one individual or couple. The necessary quantitative aspect always depends on the desired qualitative aspect.

We would respond to that question with "How much do you need and want? What kind of monthly income do you envision? What does your DREAM picture require?"

Most people are realistic about what they want and need and what they have in terms of retirement funds. But you'll have to sit down and put real numbers to practical plans. Your monthly living expenses will be so much, and then, how much will you want for traveling and other desires?

This part of painting the dream picture may not be that much fun, but it's necessary.

Another question that we will ask you is, What kind of risk are you comfortable with in your retirement accounts? If your income is okay for what you anticipate wanting to do at this point, but you have a lot of risk in your investments, you likely will have little peace with your retirement picture.

Retirement shouldn't be heavy with pressure and worry. We ask, What obstacles do you see in the way of your retirement? If you tell us you have concerns about your ability to meet your retirement goals, we know we have work to do—even if your numbers seem okay. We want to go from retirement worry, fear, and confusion, to peace and assurance of freedom.

Are you serving your money, or is your money serving you? If you're serving your money, you're probably experiencing a lot of worry, fear, and confusion. But if your money is serving you, you are experiencing the peace, freedom, and impact that retirement should be about. You have peace of mind and you have financial freedom.

LEGACY – LIFE PRINTS

Legacies don't just happen. They are planned.

Recently we were at a training event with one of our coaches, Bo Eason. Bo played in the NFL with teams like the 49ers. He played with Hall of Famer Jerry Rice! Rice is the best football receiver in history, with more touchdowns than any other player. The second-place guy is still 60 touchdowns away from Jerry's record.

Bo told a story about how Jerry accomplished his record. Every practice, the receivers would line up and run routes. Most guys would casually run the race, catch the ball, and then casually jog the ball back to the quarterback. Not Jerry. Jerry ran the route full speed. Once he caught the ball, he didn't just jog back to the quarterback. No, he turned and ran full speed all the way to the end zone—and then full speed back, every time. After a while Bo asked him why, and got this answer: "Whenever these hands touch the ball, this body goes to the end zone." Jerry does not have the all-time touchdown record by accident. His legacy wasn't by chance. Legacies are planned.

Do you want to "just retire" like some athletes "just play" in the NFL? Or do you want to be a Jerry Rice retiree? Retirement offers a life of purpose and meaning that leaves a legacy. If you want that, you are the type of person we work with.

Lifestyle is a big factor in retirement considerations. It's what most people think of in terms of retirement. But sooner or later, the questions will get around to your legacy. What do you want to pass on, and who do you want to have it? The legacy question involves both your wealth and your values and influences.

One question we like to ask is, "If you had a choice, how much (or what percent) of your estate do you want to leave to your children and grandchildren? The IRS? Charities or other organizations?"

These are the three broad categories of beneficiary around which estates are planned: family, IRS, and organizations. If you do not carefully plan to ensure that your legacy goes to the people and organizations you love, the IRS usually ends up benefiting the most.

A real retirement plan needs to ensure that you're okay as long as you're here: whether you live too long or die too soon, you're taken care of. Most people will have something left in their accounts, so it's important to figure out who's going to get it. Because truly, if you don't plan, it won't go where you want it to. You work so hard to accumulate your wealth—you may as well work a little more to plan for it to end up in the right places as well.

While you're painting your DREAM Retirement picture, think about who you want to have it on the other side. Your children? Are you concerned that your grandchildren get through college? What opportunities do you want to ensure that your loved ones can partake of fully?

What charities or organizations do you want to support? What issues are important to you?

Education? Health care? Underprivileged youth? Feeding the hungry? Clean water? What impact might you want to leave on the world in some small but tangible way?

Another part of the legacy question is the reality that too much may be going to the IRS right now. We will look and discuss options. If you had your choice, would you give your money to a charity or to the IRS? The IRS is a hidden beneficiary. The problem is that you can't often tell what portion of your legacy will go to the IRS, because estimates are based on current tax rates. We want to help you understand how taxes will impact the size of the other portions of your legacy. You can proactively work to ensure that others get what you want them to, and at the same time give less to the IRS—or eliminate them from the picture entirely.

A FINAL WORD ABOUT PAINTING

Your retirement will look different from anyone else's. The retirement of your colleague, who retires from the same company in the same year as you, will be completely different from yours. He has different goals and different priorities. Your retirement is yours, and your DREAM Retirement picture will be distinct. Don't spend a lot of time comparing retirement pictures. Your retirement is about you, the life you've lived, and the life you want to live from here on out. You can make it great!

5. What You Have – Identify Your Obstacles

Michelle's sister Kim is the youngest of the first group of kids in our family. She is determined and passionate, sensitive and loving, smart yet given to blonde moments.

For Bev's birthday one year, we decided to go to Graceland—Bev is a huge Elvis fan. Kim was living in South Carolina at the time, so she met us there. It was a great time, even for those of us not in love with Elvis! But the best memory of all came on the drive home. About halfway through the trip, Kim called us. She had just been pulled over for speeding. Here is the tale she related.

"I decided to try to drive faster on the way home after Michelle teased me all weekend about going slow. I had just sped up to 80 MPH—ten over, like Michelle said to go. Then a cop comes out of nowhere and pulls me over!

As he is getting out of his car I am wondering what I should say. So I decide to just tell the truth. I roll down my window as he is walking up, and he asks me if I am in a hurry. I reply, 'Not really. I have all day.'

He then asks if I know how fast I was going, I respond with, 'Yes—I was going 80. My sister was telling me all weekend that I was a slow poke. She said I can go ten miles over the speed limit with no problem.'

'Where is your sister?'

'On her way back to Wisconsin.'"

At this point, as she is telling us the story over the phone, we are all cracking up laughing! We assume the officer went back to his car and did the same. She got off with a warning—probably because he had just had the best laugh of his life.

Later Kim realized that the cop had not come out of nowhere. She passed what she thought was an

SUV...but was actually a patrol car. That is one obstacle you should not ignore!

Another car story occurred during her high school years. Kim was a 4.0 student—very driven and hard working. She knew what she wanted and worked hard to get it. Nothing was going to stand in her way.

However, street smarts were not her strong suit. One night she was on her way to Madison, about an hour away. She called me and asked what you should do when the engine light is red. The answer: Stop immediately!

She didn't. The light had been on for over a half hour, but she was talking on the phone to a friend and didn't pay attention to it. By the time she called, it was too late. She had burnt up the engine.

Many of the obstacles we face have warning signs. But we must look at them and pay attention if they are to help us!

Discovery process

While you are painting your DREAM Retirement picture, we will ask you if you see any obstacles standing in the way of your dream. In this second part of the DREAM Retirement Process, we dig deeper into this. We'll explore the obstacles you do seem to be aware of, and we'll look even closer to find out all the other issues that may impact your dream. Once we know what you want, we also must find out what you have to work with.

While the discovery process includes basic fact-finding, it must go deeper than merely dollars and cents. Some people want to give us a list of accounts and amounts. With this kind of information, we can give you a basic idea of your possibilities, but we can't tell you any specifics—because we just don't have the hard facts and figures to work with. We can't tell you the income you can count on or the tax liabilities you're looking at in the future, whether you are over-paying in fees or how much risk you have. We can't tell you if your current assets will provide what you want.

So we'll ask you to bring in the information you have about your retirement plans, your investments, any tax-advantaged investments you have.

ANALYSIS PROCESS

The second part of identifying obstacles is to analyze what you have—take a close look at your assets, where they are, and how they're set up.

We call this *looking for friction in your wealth engine*. When you think of your car, you know that too much of the wrong kind of friction can cause heat buildup, premature wear of parts, and erosion of fuel efficiency. These issues can lead to all sorts of other problems (remember Kim?). In the same way, when the parts of your wealth engine are not working together well, you're losing value through taxes, fees, and loss or reduction of gains. Your wealth engine is not running as efficiently as it could and should.

There are five major problems (which we call TRICKs) that contribute to friction in your wealth engine.

TAXES

Taxes are the first thing we talk about because they are fairly self-explanatory. Everybody knows they have to pay taxes and everybody hates paying taxes. Few people, however, know what they can do about paying so much tax.

> The taxpayer—that's someone who works for the federal government but doesn't have to take a civil service exam!
> Ronald Reagan

One way that taxes will affect your wealth is that your monthly expenses are post-tax, so you can't look at the bottom line in your retirement plan and investments and say that you have such and such an amount of money. Income taxes will have to come out of that tax-deferred savings and growth. You'll have to plan on having only a portion of that money to fund your retirement lifestyle.

Secondly, taxes will likely take a bite out of what you leave as your legacy. Sometimes it can be a huge bite.

And of course, the major problem with taxes is that you can only plan by calculating with current rates. Nobody knows what the tax rates will be tomorrow, so in reality, you're only giving it a calculated guess. Most people in the public that we talk to say they hope taxes stay the same, but they feel that taxes are going up. With current economic realities like our national debt, nobody really feels that taxes will go down.

> I feel honored to pay taxes in America. The thing is, I could feel just as honored at half the price!
> Arthur Godfrey

> THE ONLY DIFFERENCE BETWEEN DEATH AND TAXES IS THAT DEATH DOESN'T GET WORSE EVERY TIME CONGRESS MEETS.
> – WILL ROGERS

It can be a real slap in the face for retirees to realize how much they're losing in their 401Ks and IRAs when they go to withdraw retirement income. They've been saving up all this time because this is what they've been told to do. Then they realize that they've done well enough that their taxes aren't any lower now. They would have been lower a long time ago when they could have paid the income tax on their earnings and done something different with the money. Now they don't have the deductions they once did, and the tax rate isn't as low as they thought it would be.

Whether it is business growth, retirement income, or estate planning, taxes can be the greatest cost and hindrance to your DREAM Retirement.

Judge Learned Hand said, "There are two systems of taxation in our country: one for the informed, one for the uninformed." Most people are in the uninformed system, which means they are paying more tax than necessary. However, take heart! With a thorough look at your assets and goals, we can discover what your tax burden will likely be and plan other asset distributions to reduce and eliminate tax.

RISK

Many people we talk to say "I really just want to be more conservative. I want to make a little bit, but I certainly don't want to lose. Protecting my principal is the most important thing."

Yet they are in risky investments, because cash accounts don't make anything these days and long-term bonds can't be liquidated before maturity without interest rate risks, and they don't think anything else is available. They've been told "No guts, no glory," and "In it for the long run," and "The market will eventually come back." They're in high-risk markets and they can't sleep at night.

> Rule #1: Never lose money.
>
> Rule #2. Don't forget Rule #1.
>
> Warren Buffet

I still remember this gentleman who worked very hard and was ready to retire right before 2008. He was still getting advice to continue to try and risk, risk, risk: swing for the fences. He stayed in the market too long and entered the Great Recession with everyone else. Thus, instead of retiring in 2007, he had to work almost another decade before being able to retire.

While there may be some truth to the "No pain, no gain" mindset, when it comes to investing, the real issue is in the type of risk being taken. First, it is not always necessary to take risks to accomplish your goals. Second, unrewarded risk is never smart. Unrewarded risk is when you have more exposure to loss and less potential for gains.

Let's relate it to medicine. Let's say you must take a medication for high blood pressure, and you have two options. Both medications will provide you with the desired result—lower blood pressure. One medication has a whole page of possible side effects, while the other has only a couple. Which one would you take? That's easy. You want the one with fewer side effects.

The same is true with investing. You don't want to take on more risk to achieve the same results. And, just like your doctor will monitor your medications, your financial advisor should be monitoring your investments to make sure the gain outweighs the risk.

Types of risk

An example of unnecessary risk is when you're taking risk appropriate for aggressive growth in your portfolio when you've already achieved the wealth you want. At that point you should be focusing on preserving your money and distributing it so you can live on your retirement funds. You wanted that aggressiveness when you were younger, accumulating your wealth—but now involvement in the more volatile market is not necessary. It could lose you wealth, since you don't have the time horizon to recover from downturns.

Sometimes the fees and taxes you pay are also unnecessary. We'll explore that when we look at your wealth engine.

Another example of unrewarded risk is when a fund is taking above-average risk for a below-average return. You're taking too much risk when the market is down but not getting proportional gain when it's up. This is unnecessary.

Risk numbers

Part of the problem in trying to manage risk is that the definition of *conservative* is different for everyone. When you tell your advisor you want to be conservative, he will tell you, "You are already being conservative." That is true—by his standards. But you are still less conservative than you would like to be! Your investments have more risk than you desire. By nature, stockbrokers are not likely to be exceptionally conservative. Their definition of *conservative* may be much riskier than your retiree definition.

We'll sit down with you and examine the risk you currently have, compared to the level you are comfortable with. How much of your investments are at risk? A lot of risk or a little risk? How much of your principal is protected against loss? Then we'll examine how much of that risk is necessary, and what the potential rewards are for each kind of risk.

Tools are available that will look at your own preferences and comfort levels to determine what your risk number is—much like determining your ideal "sleep number" on those adjustable beds. Then the tool will examine your portfolio to determine the actual level of risk you're taking with your accounts set as they are. It's a tangible number you can see and use for hard comparisons, instead of a vague category like "conservative" or "aggressive."

Suppose your risk number comes up low, say 33 on the scale from 1 to 99. What if your portfolio score comes back at 70? Now we know that you're taking way more risk than you want. Or what if you have a risk number of 50 and a portfolio score of 50? You're right where you should be in terms of risk vs. protected principal. Every individual will have their own risk comfort score, and each retirement portfolio can be adjusted accordingly.

We can forecast with this tool, putting real numbers to likely loss or gain over the next six months. Someone might think they're okay with a 10% loss on their bottom line. But when they put a quantifiable dollar amount on that potential, they may not be okay any longer. Ten percent might sound tolerable—but $200,000 out of $2,000,000? Maybe not.

BRING IT ALL TOGETHER

Too many times, advisors focus on just one of these risk factors and not the other. They will have high performing funds, but too high a risk number—or the right risk number, but poorly performing funds. The point of this is to be able to bring appropriate correction to the amounts and types of investment accounts your money is in, so that you'll have the desired outcome. You can see clearly that you're gaining appropriately and not losing where you don't have to or can't afford to. You can weed out the poorly returning funds and get that money into better performing funds.

Some risk may be necessary to create your DREAM Retirement plan, but not all risk is created equal. Too much unrewarded and unnecessary risk will put friction into your wealth engine.

INVESTMENT MIX

Investment mix is closely related to risk. It's about the types of funds you're invested in. People talk about the importance of diversification, but we frequently find that people think they're well diversified, while they aren't diversified at all.

What we mean is this: you could have 50 different holdings, but if all 50 work the same way you are not any safer. If all your funds move up and down at the same time under the same market influences, you're still at risk. People say, "I don't want to put all my eggs in the same basket." This is smart. So they pick a lot of different stocks to invest in—a lot of different "baskets." But then they go and put all their baskets in the same truck and watch it go down the road. What happens if that truck hits a bad bump? Every single basket goes flying. All the eggs break.

To counteract this, you can select some investments that are principal-protected. This means there's never loss of what you put in, only gains. Next, pick stocks that have a variety of responses to different market stresses. Part of this strategy might also be picking different fund managers who operate with diverse investing styles.

As alluded to in the Risk section, many more investment choices exist than most people realize. There are different types of performances you can select to achieve the diversification and risk levels you need.

Put your eggs in different baskets, but make sure those baskets are all in different trucks taking different routes. This way you can minimize the loss that shows up in your wealth engine when you're not truly diversified.

Cost

When we sit down with clients, we also take a good look at the fees they are paying for their account management. A reasonable fee for responsible account management is proper, but it's also important to be sure you're not overpaying, or paying for services you aren't receiving, or paying for benefits or riders you don't need. So many people don't have any idea of the fees they're paying.

Most of the time, fees are hidden and can't be easily discerned. Unneeded services and products that are being paid for can't be easily identified in all the fine print. Individuals don't know where to look or even the questions to ask. And when they call to ask what the fees are, they're given a basic fee, but not all the possible fees they could be charged. Sometimes this is because the phone was answered by a customer service rep who hasn't been trained completely and just doesn't have a clue themselves.

However, sometimes this is an intentional practice by companies. One of our clients had a 401K, which has more obscure fees. We asked him to request a certain disclosure from his broker so we could dig deeper, and gave him the legal name of the disclosure to ask for. But his broker sent him the wrong disclosure. We felt that was very intentional misdirection.

So one thing we'll do is look over your accounts to identify the costs and fees you're paying out. Sometimes those fees can't be taken off, like line items on a purchase order where you decide not to buy everything that got written up. Some of those fees you're stuck with, because you're using some other portion of a service that's attached. But some of those fees can be eliminated once you know what they are. There's no sense in leaking wealth in fees and charges you don't have to pay. It's not a matter of, "You should be paying only this much for this service or that much for that product." It's more a matter of getting value and service for the fees you are paying.

KNOWLEDGE GAPS

"You don't know what you don't know."

It's simple, but very profound.

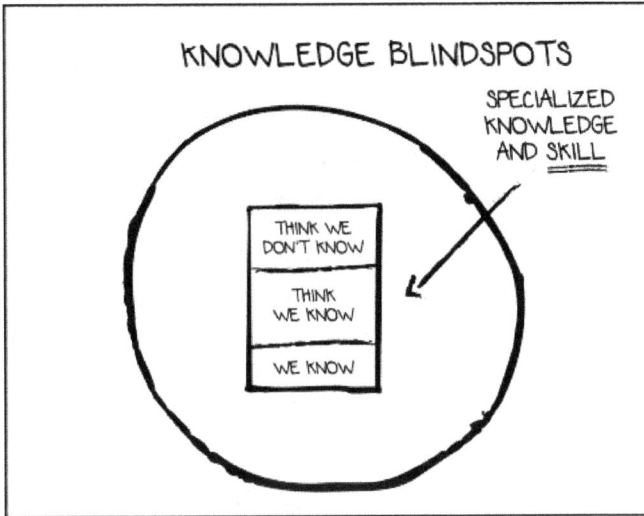

One thing that is important for retirees and investors to understand is the reality that there are probably a lot more options out there available than they know—and more than their current advisor may know or have access to. For each of us, there are things we know, things we think we know but might not actually know, and things we think we don't know. And then there are the things we don't know—concepts and realities we don't even know exists.

Those who are most successful in reaching their dream retirement goals are those who take the time to explore all the offerings out there. Instead of assuming their advisor has their best interests at heart and will bring up the best options available, they take the time to look around and learn if there are better ways out there to maximize their wealth.

Most advisors representing major investment houses have access to only a limited type and number of services and products. They operate only in a Green Money arena, or only in a Red Money arena (more on this later). The nature of their primary offerings prevents them from having access to other types of investments that yield different growth potential and different risks. But it's important to know, as you're aware of your goals and the risk you're comfortable with, that there are many options available that can directly address your situation better than others. Independent financial planners who are not tied to a specific brokerage will likely have better knowledge of more offerings. They can help you tailor the plan that you need according to your desired return and acceptable risk.

Sometimes your advisor may be highly skilled in wealth accumulation, but not as proficient in preserving wealth and efficiently converting assets to retirement lifestyle funds. Remember that your needs at age 60 are different than they were at age 30. You can't risk the loss now that you might have experienced and recovered from in 2008.

Another knowledge gap that people can get caught in is being swayed by what is promoted in the media. Radio and television and printed advertisements are full of opinions that seem to be sound and trustworthy. The sad truth is that much of the information put out there is not based on solid facts and figures. It's frequently very misleading, and sometimes the people hawking products and services don't even understand things themselves.

The media is not there to educate you for your best interests. It's there to sell you stuff. There's an agenda behind getting a particular service or product into the public eye, and that agenda is not your best financial interests. Yet so many people looking at retirement listen to these ads. Some bring a magazine page in to us and want to do this or that, because it sounds like a good idea. They don't stop to consider what might be behind the advertisement. That tool may not truly apply to what they want or need. It might be disastrous.

We acknowledge that a little bit of true wisdom usually exists in every potential offering. But that wisdom must be sorted out of the mass of information about that offering. And the information must be gleaned out of the words and noise out there, all shouting that they're the truth.

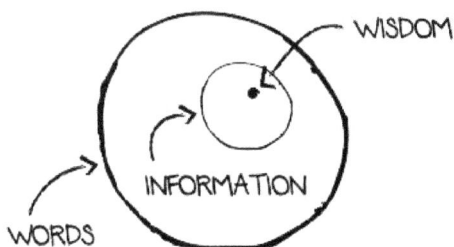

LOOKING FOR WISDOM FROM MEDIA, INTERNET AND FRIENDS

WISDOM

INFORMATION

WORDS

This includes popular money gurus and TV personalities who tout this or that method or product. We think of a couple of individuals who have fantastic debt-free lifestyle models that they teach all over the world. But we cringe when we hear about their investment recommendations, because they're not based on the reality that we see every day. There's no argument that they know what they're talking about in terms of eliminating personal debt and getting your financial lifestyle under control.

Nevertheless, their understanding of wealth accumulation is a bit limited.

At this point, you may be alarmed by the realization that you have some gaping holes in your retirement plan, or other problems in your wealth engine.

The book of Proverbs says that there is wisdom in a multitude of counselors. Wise people understand this and do not shy away from ideas or tools that are new to them. They go back over their situation and seek second opinions to enhance their situation and expand their knowledge. They are able to eliminate friction in their wealth engine.

At the same time, you should not expect yourself to do all the research and become an investing expert. The point is, find a good partnership with someone who has access to a wide range of tools, someone who will also sit down with you to pinpoint exactly what you want and help you tailor the best possible plan.

Part 3 of the DREAM Retirement Process is tailoring that best possible plan for you. What you need is to create your DREAM Blueprint.

6. What You Need – Create Your DREAM Blueprint

When we were kids, one of our favorite things to do was look at home design books. We would rent them from the library and plan our dream house. Most of the books I remember also included floor plans. They were architect design books—not so much the cosmetic design as the layout design. We would find a design we liked and then dream about the house, from our future families to how everything would look.

I remember I always liked the designs with the master bedroom set apart from the kids' bedrooms. I would dream about my handsome husband and how I would want private time without our beautiful kids right next door.

When I first decided to buy a house I was single, but still had some of these thoughts in my head. So I chose a house in which the master bedroom was downstairs and the other bedrooms upstairs.

However, this did not turn out to be the right design for me. When I brought baby Asa home several years later, no way did I want him sleeping upstairs so far away from me! Instead, he slept with me. Those bedrooms upstairs were rarely used. Even when Angel stayed, she wanted to sleep with me—so only Anthony and any other visitors ever slept upstairs.

In the second house I bought, all the bedrooms are upstairs together. Asher sleeps in his room most of the time, but it's only a few feet away from me—not all the way through the house and up the stairs!

Sometimes the blueprint we design at one point in our life ends up not being needed or desired in the end.

What should happen now?

So far we have painted your DREAM Retirement picture and seen exactly how you want your retirement to look. You've sketched out the lifestyle you want while you're living and the legacy you want to leave when you're gone.

We've looked at your wealth engine to identify where you might be leaking wealth. Now it's time to see if *what you have* and *what you want* will match up. Most people have the sneaky suspicion that what they want and what they have don't quite line up, so it's time to create the blueprint for a new picture.

While we may use some of the same discovery tools and investing tools for all our clients, each of the DREAM Retirement Blueprints we help create is as unique as the individuals and couples who come through our door. Each dream is different; each set of assets and obstacles is different; and so each blueprint will be completely unique from every other blueprint.

If you were to build a house from scratch, you'd start by drawing up your blueprint with the rooms you want, noting things like elevations, windows, and outdoor access. You would draw up what you want—what you think would be the most practical and satisfactory—because you would have spent some time thinking about your desires.

All home blueprints include common elements: walls, doorways, windows, plumbing, HVAC. Likewise, your DREAM Retirement Blueprint will have some aspects in common with others' blueprints. One of the essentials is your retirement income plan—the plan that will allow you the lifestyle income you want and, hopefully, the legacy impact you want to leave.

We'll address any of the friction issues we've discovered in your wealth engine. We can eliminate some costs, rearrange investments to get better tax benefits, or put some capital away in principal-protected assets to assure a minimum certain amount of income down the road. We'll take the stress out of your retirement expectations.

The thing about blueprints is that you can change your mind midway through the project. You can step back and say "No, we don't need that room anymore," or "These windows need to go all the way to the ceiling in the great room. We want all the light we can get." Things in your life might change;

aspects of your DREAM Retirement picture might change if you want something different. We can change the blueprint accordingly, since it is always flexible and customizable.

7. DREAM Blueprint Case Studies

As we've mentioned, every single DREAM Retirement picture is unique. Nobody's retirement looks like anyone else's. While each retirement plan may deal with the same issues of risk, taxation, guaranteed income, and so on, every plan is designed to meet a specific set of desires and outcomes. The case studies below simply illustrate some of the different concerns that we've encountered and reveal how we dealt with each one effectively.

The Saxtons – Legacy and taxes

The Saxtons had gotten into the dairy equipment industry in the early 1980's. William had started in with service calls, and in a few years was repping locally for a dairy equipment manufacturer. They had their tight moments—particularly in 2008—but overall they did okay.

A few years ago, the Saxtons came in to speak with us. They had handed the business off to their daughter and son-in-law and wanted to secure their overall plan. They also wanted to see if they could do anything to reduce their taxes.

When we went through the DREAM Retirement Process, it became very clear that two of their major goals were traveling and charitable giving. They wanted to go back to the "Old Country," look up quite a few families, and see the places of origin for ancestors on both sides. They also intended to leave each of the three kids (and eleven grandkids) in as good a financial place as possible.

Mr. and Mrs. Saxton said they thought they were comfortable with their income level, their risk, and their investments, but they agreed that we should run the risk numbers. It turned out they were taking a bit more risk than necessary. Even though their income was fine, they did have some losing and underperforming stocks. The Blueprint we created for them included a process to weed out the losers, adjust the risk level, and implement a process to manage and monitor their portfolio on an ongoing basis.

One of the underperforming funds was a stock that, had they sold it, would have given them a huge hit for capital gains. It was over a half million in one company—fairly risky by any standard. Part of the Blueprint was to transfer that stock into a capital gains avoidance trust. Within that trust they were able to sell the stock without paying capital gains. This gave them an income tax deduction of nearly $90,000, and it also guaranteed another $25,000 in income for their retirement. They were happy about that!

When we took a close look at their taxes, they found about what they expected: a quarter of their wealth would be going to the IRS in taxes upon their passing. They rankled at the idea of the IRS getting upwards of $500,000.

Another part of the legacy they wanted to pass on was *the value of charitable giving*. They wanted their kids and grandkids to practice giving in a real way. Most people plan to give to their kids, then have their kids give it away. But nobody gets any kind of tax break doing this. The IRS will get virtually half of those retirement accounts in hidden estate tax.

Instead of using this method, the Saxtons left their IRAs to a family-controlled charity. After their deaths, the people in the family-controlled charity will be able to make charitable gifts each year, carrying on the process of giving that their parents wanted. And these gifts remain tax free. Dad and Mom reinforced their value of giving back while saving taxes—one of the reasons they came to us in the first place.

When their DREAM Blueprint was complete, the Saxtons were able to give upwards of $5 million to their kids and grandkids, about 2 million to charity, and nothing to the IRS. They told us, "We really have confidence and clarity of mind now. We know that what we have in place will guarantee our wishes, and we're free to do our traveling and retirement fun." They have greater peace of mind and complete freedom now. They thought they were okay, and they truly were okay—but now they are more than okay. They can live their DREAM Retirement with confidence and peace that they will also leave a legacy.

Ben – Risk

One of the client stories we tell again and again is Ben's, because it is so heartbreaking. It encapsulates so much of why we do what we do. Ben had been planning to retire around 2008. He'd wanted to retire at age 60, but his whole portfolio was in high risk. When the bear market hit, he lost half of everything. He ended up delaying his retirement because he no longer felt he could create the lifestyle he wanted after suffering this loss.

He came to us after the crash, probably in 2011. By then, he had regained a good portion of what he had lost, but he was concerned about another market downturn. His advisor had told him he was in good shape before, and then he lost big. Although he didn't want that to happen again, he didn't know what else to do. And his current advisor wasn't giving him any help.

Ben attended one of our special events and decided to come have a conversation with us. Primarily, what he wanted was some type of guarantee on his money. He knew his DREAM Retirement couldn't survive another hit like 2008. He would be able to retire, yes, but not fund his desired retirement lifestyle.

Ben's DREAM Blueprint included a good portion of his portfolio being transferred into Green Money accounts, which gave him some growth potential linked to the market with no risk of loss. These accounts also had guarantees for retirement income so he could *know* he would have the income he needed to fund his DREAM Retirement lifestyle. As part of his DREAM Blueprint, we left some of his assets in the market so he could continue growing his portfolio—but we also implemented a management and monitoring process aligned with his desired risk level.

It took a long time for him to recover from the loss he suffered in 2008. And he had to set aside so many plans he'd made around his retirement. Plans with his family and plans around his passion for photography had to go on hold for a few years. But thanks to the DREAM Retirement Process, Ben retired last year and start living his DREAM! He built that wall and moat of guarantees around himself and his family, ensuring his retirement plans and his legacy will never be derailed again. He told us that after going through the DREAM Retirement Process, he has financial peace of mind that he never thought was possible!

The Larsons – Guaranteed income and risk

The Larsons, successful small business owners, were already retired when they came to one of our events. They came because they are always looking to increase their knowledge—they credit their success to their willingness to learn and openness to apply new ideas. They had not thought about the possibility of unseen obstacles to their plan, and decided it was something they should investigate a little more. We proceeded through the DREAM Retirement Process and uncovered some big problems in their wealth engine.

Most of their portfolio was in high risk, and the largest portion of it was in a variable annuity that provided guaranteed income. The guaranteed income part sounded great—until they realized that the income was guaranteed only for Mr. Larson's lifetime, and not for Mrs. Larson's. That, coupled with the high-risk investments, might well have been disastrous! If their accounts did not perform at a high level, the principal would be reduced by the income taken. This means the amount to be transferred to Mrs. Larson in the event of her husband's passing would continue to decrease. Mrs. Larson was about five years younger than Mr. Larson, and (statistically speaking) women tend to outlive men. If they remained on their current plan, not too many years down the road Mrs. Larson's death benefit would be insufficient to fund the retirement lifestyle she enjoyed. There would be less income from the retirement income plan he'd set up, in addition to less from Social Security.

This was not what they expected, and certainly not what they wanted. It was time to re-design their retirement. The DREAM Blueprint we created allowed them to get the money out of that variable annuity into another financial product with even better guaranteed income. This product would last for them both for the rest of their lives, regardless of whether their spouse was still living or not. The other portion of their portfolio was put into a more conservative investment that would be managed and monitored. That portion of the portfolio was there if they needed money over and above the guaranteed income (like to replace the car or repair the house). This was what they wanted. It returned them to the comfort level they'd been at before we sat down to look closely at their wealth engine.

"The DREAM Retirement Process saved me from the poorhouse," commented Mrs. Larson. "We both worked hard to create a successful business and we both want to live our DREAM Retirement. Without this process, we might have faced disaster without even realizing it was around the corner."

The Petersons – Having a plan

The Petersons were a hardworking couple who started with technical training right out of high school and worked their entire careers each in a single trade. John was an electrician, and Jean retired after being recognized for 35 years of service as a court reporter in the same county court system. John wanted to retire soon as well.

Over the years, John and Jean had accumulated a healthy portfolio. They asked their financial representative if he was sure they had enough to retire. Jean wanted to spend time with her gardening club and book clubs, and John liked to craft wood furniture at their summer home in Minnesota near the grandkids. They didn't have big travel plans; their goals were modest and comfortable.

However, their advisor did not answer their query satisfactorily. He just told them "Yeah, yeah, you'll be fine." Even at their repeated requests for concrete numbers, he only replied, "You'll be fine; don't worry about it."

By the time they visited us, The Petersons were turned off by their advisor. They still weren't sure if John should go ahead and retire. As always, we began by having them paint their DREAM Retirement picture. We found out what their goals were, what their ideal retirement income would be, and their feelings on risk, taxes and legacy.

After gaining a clear picture of what their DREAM Retirement should look like, we gathered information about their current situation. Then we started creating their DREAM Blueprint. It turned out that they would easily be able to generate the amount of retirement income they wanted. However, a few obstacles still stood in their way. First, they had way more risk than they were comfortable with. Second, they had no idea how to create retirement income that would last.

As part of their DREAM Blueprint, we moved some of their assets around, both reducing risk and securing protected income. Because John wasn't yet old enough to claim Social Security, we had to find alternate income sources for a few years. In the end, we showed them step by step where their income would come from over the next 30 years. John and Jean could finally see that their assets would indeed allow them to retire and do the things they wanted.

"This is exactly what we wanted," Jean repeated more than once as we worked through the DREAM Retirement Process with them. The report's concrete helped them feel so much better about retirement. "This is exactly what we wanted: Someone to sit down, show us where our income will come from, and then tell us we are going to be okay. Now we have a plan."

THE SMITHS – EARLY RETIREMENT

The Smiths owned a cheese company and had a substantial, well-performing portfolio. They'd worked hard, added a few specialty cheeses, and ended up doing very well in business. At 65, Belle was getting ready to retire. Bert, six years younger than Belle, thought he was going to have to work a few more years.

Bert and Belle wanted to visit the ten children they sponsored through various ministries around the world. They'd been to see each child at least once already, and were ready to make another visit.

They also wanted to spend their retirement free time working at their church's summer youth outreaches, unwed mothers' home, and after-school tutoring program. We joked with them that they were essentially retiring so they could go to work. This couple was very committed to helping youngsters wherever they could.

We sat down to examine their portfolio. At the end of the DREAM Retirement Process, we ended up taking out about 75% of the risk and establishing it to set a regular income that let them do their traveling and community work. After that, it turned out that Bert needed to work only three more years instead of the six he had anticipated. They were able to sell the company, and on the income plan they'd established, they went to see their children and pour themselves into their community.

"The DREAM Retirement process has allowed us to really live our legacy out in retirement and also ensure that our impact will be felt for years after we are gone," Bert and Belle wrote in a thank-you note. "Now we are confident that we will have the freedom to accomplish our retirement goals and the peace of knowing our 'kids' will be the benefactors of all our hard work, leaving Uncle Sam out of the equation."

THE JONESES – BETTER RETURN, LONG-TERM CARE, AND THE FAMILY FARM

The Joneses were the complete opposite of Ben: instead of too much market risk, they had too much purchasing power risk. Since they did not like market risk, they placed all their assets in cash-type accounts that were making little to nothing. When they came in to have a conversation with us, they didn't know what their options were for greater gains. Working through the DREAM Retirement process brought a couple other issues to light.

Their DREAM Retirement Blueprint included transferring some of their assets to Green Money solutions that allowed them to gain triple the interest while keeping their principal risk-free. They were quite happy to be making more money without taking on market risk!

Another issue the Joneses' DREAM Blueprint needed to address was long-term care. Because David had a degenerative movement disorder, he couldn't qualify for a long-term care policy. We accessed some tools with long-term care riders that can double income for a five-year period. By moving some of their funds to these products, they gained not only a better return but also peace of mind. If David does need long-term care down the road, they have help with those bills. It won't pay 100% of the care—but it will take a significant burden off their retirement income.

The last thing we addressed in their DREAM Retirement Blueprint was keeping their family homestead in the family. The Joneses' children couldn't take over the property and maintain it on a regular basis, but they wanted to have access to the home and the land for their fall family hunting trips. A little work with an estate planning lawyer brought David's sister into the picture to take care of the homestead, but keep it available for the kids during the hunting seasons. David was deeply relieved that the homestead didn't have to leave the family.

"We were doing fine before we went through the DREAM Retirement process," commented Mr.

Jones, "but we wanted to be more than fine. We wanted to address these issues and didn't know how to do so. We now feel that we are set up in a much better way to allow us to continue living our DREAM Retirement regardless of what may happen and leave our legacy to our children."

8. What To Do – Implement Action Steps

DON'T LET YOUR LEARNING LEAD TO
KNOWLEDGE, OR YOU'LL BECOME A FOOL.
LET YOUR LEARNING LEAD TO ACTION,
AND YOU CAN BECOME WEALTHY.

– JIM ROHN

COMMITMENT TO CHANGE

I (Michelle) used to frequently take kids on survival-type camping trips called Nikos. "Niko" means overcomer, and the purpose of these trips was mission preparation and leadership training. The kids knew they were going camping and hiking—that's all. They knew nothing of the exact schedule. In fact, the weekend itinerary was revealed to them about five minutes before the action commenced. To start off every trip we told the story of an old army officer who oversaw prisoner executions. Before each execution, he would give the prisoner a choice: the firing squad or an unknown black door.

Every time the prisoner chose the firing squad; every time this old officer hung his head and walked away. Observing these events, a young officer approached him and asked, "Sir, you always give the prisoners a choice. And when they choose the firing squad, you seem disappointed. What is behind the black door?" The old officer gazed at him and replied, "Behind that black door is freedom—but few have the courage to choose it."

Now is your time for courage. This is where the rubber meets the road. So far, you've spent time thinking and dreaming about what retirement means to you. The details look attractive now that you've written them down: the travel, the playing, the golf, the gardening, the volunteering, the friendships, the family time. You've decided the specifics of the impact and legacy you want to leave around when you're gone.

We've dug down to find out what you have and identified both the known and unknown obstacles you face.

We've put together the blueprint needed to create your DREAM Retirement. It's all out there on paper. It's encouraging, exciting even.

Now it's time to implement. To change anything—your health, your wealth, your weight—you must make three commitments: time, money, and mindset.

For instance, if you want to get in shape, you must take time to work out. You might have to spend money on healthy foods and a gym membership. And you need to change how you think. Otherwise, you will never commit to rise early and exercise, nor eat the salad instead of the bacon cheeseburger.

Time

It might take a bit of time for you to absorb and understand exactly what's involved in the changes to your existing financial plan. Ask your questions and be sure you're satisfied. Plan on meeting with the various professionals who will put the parts of the big picture into place. Plan on stopping in to open accounts and sign documents.

Money

You're aware of the fees and costs associated with your investments so far, so the fact that changes come with fees is no surprise. But as we move forward into implementing the larger pieces of your whole income and legacy, there may be some other costs involved.

There will be fees associated with some of the legal documents likely needing to be executed. There may be fees involved for creating a plan, and there will probably be fees to manage the investment portfolio going forward.

The flip side is that not changing also comes at a price. The question is, "Which will cost you more?"

Mindset

> THE SIGNIFICANT PROBLEMS WE FACE CANNOT
> BE SOLVED AT THE SAME LEVEL OF THINKING

Probably the most significant (and potentially the hardest) point of change will be an aspect of your perspective, your mindset. Some of the tools, tactics and strategies that could be part of your DREAM Blueprint may be new to you. These may be exactly what you need to meet your goals and live your DREAM, but they may also be strategies you are unfamiliar with.

The *status quo bias* is the unfortunate reality that people will often stay with what they have, no matter how bad the performance—because there are afraid to make a change.

Change can be hard. Change can be scary. To make a change, you must first have a change mindset.

Successful people understand that they don't know everything. Therefore, they value the specialists who do know, who can glean the speck of wisdom for their situation from the information available, separating it from the glut of opinions and facts and misinformation out there. They know when it's time to trust someone else's wisdom. When it comes to bettering their own situation, they know they need to learn something new; otherwise, nothing will change.

A MAP, A GPS, OR A PERSONAL GUIDE?

The book *Three Cups of Tea* is about a mountain climber who was inspired to build schools in Afghanistan and Pakistan. His source of inspiration? An encounter with impoverished villagers.

Most mountain climbers do not require much assistance to ascend the mountain. Rather, the descent forces them to ask for help. Such was the case in this story. On one mountain-climbing expedition, the author got lost a few times as he tried to descend. His porter (or Sherpa) had to find him and guide him. He ended up stopping at a local village to recuperate, which led to his life-changing encounter with the local villagers. However, this encounter would never have taken place were it not for the climber's guide down the mountain.

Retirement planning has been likened to mountain climbing. The truth is that you can get up the mountain just fine. It's relatively easy to go up. You just need to understand best practices for planning routes and taking breaks, how to pack and set up camp.

Accumulating wealth is the same. Most people are familiar with the concepts of saving, interest, and investing. If business is good and you manage your finances such that your bottom line is always in the black and you're putting cash away, you can get up the mountain satisfactorily.

However, getting back down safely is not so easy. Once you've enjoyed the exhilaration of reaching the summit, you need a guide who is intimately familiar with the dangers and step-by-step processes of getting down. You need to keep from getting lost or succumbing to cold or dehydration or poor oxygen or disorientation. You're fatigued, and those paths don't look the same going down as they did going up. Every footfall is just a step away from a tumble that could end your life.

Wise mountain climbers know this. They don't depend on their own wits to get back down. They want the knowledge of someone who has made this trek before and who is intimately acquainted with the best paths, the hidden dangers, and the incoming storm clouds. They hire local Sherpas for this, men who grew up near the mountain and have led climbers many times before.

Similarly, you have now made it to the top of Mount Accumulation. Time for you to descend. You need to start converting your assets to create a retirement income stream that funds your DREAM Retirement and allows you to live and leave a legacy.

If you were on the top of the mountain, would you want to be handed a map with directions written on it, a GPS to give you step-by-step instructions, or a guide to go with you?

If you're looking to the advisor you worked with for saving and increasing your wealth, remember that while this individual might excel at wealth accumulation, he or she might not possess the best knowledge or tools for converting your savings to retirement income. Though the advisor might have some basic ideas, his expertise is wealth building—not wealth distribution. The potential situations are simply too complex for a general advisor to be able to speak to each one thoroughly. If your advisor is attached to a single investment house, he will have only a few products or services with which to manage your money and, therefore, a limited range of disbursement options. He won't be familiar with potential tax situations, nor able to set up appropriate plans even if he's aware of them and able to tell you about them. The best he can do is give you a map or maybe a GPS.

You need is a guide, a specialist, someone who's familiar with the terrain and potential pitfalls and the best approaches. More than that, you want a specialist who is part of a team of specialists: CPAs, tax specialists, attorneys, and advisors. Beware of the generalist who tells you they can do it all in regards to your estate and retirement planning. He's going to be a jack of all trades, master of none. Look for someone who knows where the answers are and who is willing to outsource. Look for someone who has a network of contacts in every appropriate profession, someone who may not have all the answers, but who knows people who do.

You wouldn't trust a heart issue to your family physician, would you? Of course not. As soon as your general practitioner tells you he's concerned about your heart, you're on the phone with the best cardiac doctor he can recommend. When you're young and healthy, you can get away with seeing a general practitioner on only rare occasions. But when you get older and your body stops cooperating the way it used to, you look for specialists familiar with your issues.

In football, would you expect even the most skilled quarterback to carry the championship by himself? He needs a strong D line and a strong O line. He needs quick and agile receivers downfield. He needs a good coaching and training staff. You do too.

We believe in teams. Bertram Financial strongly specializes in retirement income and business owners, and we bring in experts to address the different aspects of each blueprint. For example, we have a team of tax specialists, because the tax code is 70,000 pages long. One tax expert isn't going to cut it. Our estate planning attorney brings in his own team to work the more advanced charitable designs. No one person can possibly know everything.

We want to be your authority on the matter, but not the sole expert. We're an authority because of our familiarity with retirement planning issues, solutions, integration, and implementation to secure a successful retirement. Though we might not be experts in every aspect, we recognize when we need an expert—and we know who they are.

Follow-up and review

Many (if not most) brokers and financial services reps focus on the next client as soon as they've signed you. They've courted you and convinced you to buy—now you're on your own. You have to make sense of the annual reports and decide if you need to make changes. And when you schedule an in-person appointment, your broker hasn't even opened your file in advance of the meeting.

How confidence-inspiring is that relationship? Can you make sense of the annual reports by yourself? Are you good with that level of monitoring while you wonder if you're getting the gain you need?

Or, upon signing up for financial planning services, would you prefer to receive a schedule of follow-up and review meetings you can count on?

Investment performance must be monitored. No stock or stocks will serve you perfectly forever, so it's good to expect some re-assignment of assets. Your wealth management plan should be reviewed and checked to see if any of your retirement goals or needs have shifted enough that you need to make change. And, most importantly, you may need to review the plan periodically just to refresh your memory and keep you on track—like Richard.

Richard had a plan set up that guaranteed him good income. However, after a stroke, his needs changed.

Some of the change was ongoing physical concerns, necessitating a switch in some assets for better access to funds. The most significant post-stroke change was his poorer judgment in personal finances. He had been strict with his spending, but after his stroke, he became a bit more careless. Occasionally, he calls us wanting "just a wee bit more"—his words for a big spending spree.

So we go over the plan we set up with Richard. We show him how the money in his accounts will be enough only if he sticks with the plan. His income is certainly adequate to fund his desired lifestyle (most of the time). We also review the plan with him to check that it's doing the best it can, and reiterate that he'll be fine only if he sticks with the plan. Richard agrees that his choices need to be scaled back, and so far, the plan has worked. It just takes a little review periodically.

Most individuals and couples we work with are fine with the review schedule that we establish for everyone. However, we recognize that the best care and service follows your schedule, and so every review schedule can be altered to best suit you.

Your financial goals are long-term, playing out over time. They should be handled in a long-term relationship, not in a few minimally-considered transactions. This is your life, your retirement, and it's as important to us as it is to you.

9. Benefits of the DREAM Retirement Process

Do you remember your first kiss?

We were recently at a training event and they asked everyone this question. I (Michelle) immediately thought not of my first kiss, but my first *real* kiss. There is a difference!

When I think about the first real kiss I still get tingles. I remember exactly where I was, how it happened, the details of the night. I remember the rush or excitement, the sensation. And I remember thinking: Now this is what kissing is all about!

My first kiss did none of that. I can't even remember exactly where or how it happened. It was a blah event. I might not have even consciously thought it, but somewhere there was the idea that kissing is not what it was cracked up to be.

Then the real first kiss happened and WOW!

That is a picture of the DREAM Retirement process. It takes the blah out of planning and turns it into a WOW!

WHAT DOES FINANCIAL FREEDOM MEAN TO YOU?

There it is, the DREAM Retirement Process.

How do you feel now?

There are three things we want most for you at the other end of working through the DREAM Retirement Process.

First, we want peace of mind for you. Do you remember the Whites in the first chapter? Their situation was exactly the opposite of peace of mind. Yet (as you saw in many of Chapter 7's case studies) at the end of the DREAM Retirement Process, all our clients say in one way or another that *they feel more peace*. They have peace in knowing that a solid plan was in place. They feel secure that their goals will be met and that they are protected from the next bear market. They have the confidence to live their DREAM Retirement, because the DREAM

Retirement Process assures them that their financial matters are satisfactory.

Your retirement wealth doesn't have to be a guessing game, with your fingers crossed every time you open your statements.

You can take action to discern your assets, their growth, and improvement strategies. How can your money be managed for maximum wealth? You can minimize and eliminate loss from taxes and fees and downturns. You can be confident and look forward to your DREAM Retirement with the knowledge that it's secure.

Second, we want financial freedom for you. Freedom means different things to different people. Maybe financial freedom means you're free to stop working. You might intend to work for a lot longer, but because you want to—not because you have to.

Financial freedom is being able to do what you want to do, when you want to do it. You're in control.

You're free to spend your time working to benefit others. Maybe freedom means you can use your money to influence and support issues you feel are important. Your needs are taken care of, and now you can pour your energy and resources into helping others—doing your part to make a bit of the world a brighter, better place. You can send your grandkids to school, or fund that scholarship to your alma mater, or help campaign to get the best candidate into office.

Like the Petersons (who had a good nest egg but needed a solid plan) or the Smiths (who planned and worked to retire and pour themselves into their "kids" all over the world), your retirement dreams and desires are very personal and important to you. We want to do what we can to help you reach that point of financial freedom.

Finally, we want to help you make an impact and secure your legacy.

> For we are God's masterpiece. He has created us anew in Christ Jesus, so we can do the good

things he planned for us long ago.
– Ephesians 2:10

We believe that everyone was created for a purpose, and that the world would be a better place if everyone did what they were created to do. We want to help you make your desired impact in your family and community. Retirement brings you a new opportunity to touch your world. You have more knowledge, skills and time than ever before—so use them to do what you are were created to do!

A colleague of ours named Jim has invested his retirement into Haiti through his organization Operation Go. Drawing upon a lifetime of business expertise, he partnered with a local pastor to create an entrepreneurial center. Together they train Haitians to start and run their own businesses, as well as become effective community leaders.

Jim's organization works to take many Americans on mission trips so they can experience life from another viewpoint, encouraging them to use their passions to serve globally. Operation Go is also deeply involved in caring for orphans in Haiti by sending monthly support to four orphanages. Jim's work helps provide food, basic supplies, and school materials for the kids. He is living the retirement dream and benefiting untold numbers of people too!

> One of the most common characteristics of a person who is nearing the end of the first half is that unquenchable desire to move from success to significance. After the first half of building a career and trying to become financially secure, we'd like to do something in the second half that is more meaningful—something that rises above perks and paychecks into the stratosphere of significance.
>
> – Bob Buford, in *Halftime: Changing Your Game Plan from Success to Significance*

You can plan now so that your legacy will indeed go the way you want it to go. Your wealth and values will go to your kids, your grandchildren, and the organizations you champion—not to the IRS or to estate, probate, and civil lawyers.

Only with a good structure in place can you be sure of leaving peace instead of strife for your heirs. I'm reminded of when Joe Robbie, the owner of the Miami Dolphins, passed away. His son Dan said that because of how his dad left matters, the kids were put in a tough situation. You don't want your children to say that.

> WHAT MAN REALLY FEARS IS NOT SO MUCH EXTINCTION, BUT EXTINCTION WITH INSIGNIFICANCE.
>
> – ERNEST BECKER

The DREAM Retirement process doesn't just help you live a rich and full life now. It also ensures that you will leave a legacy behind. It's strange and hard to think about being gone. Nobody wants to think about living life and then think about one day being gone. But when you consider the legacy you can leave in terms of your wealth, your values, and your influence, you can begin to envision the good you can leave behind. You can be at peace with your decisions that will have an ongoing influence after you yourself have lived your best life.

PART III.
DREAM EXTRAS

10. Business Owners

Businesses are the lifeblood of a community, providing jobs and services that are a vital part of the economy and society. At the same time, business owners are penalized the most when it comes to taxes.

We know business owners are working toward their DREAM Retirement and creating their DREAM business along the way. Every business owner needs to check their wealth engine for friction. The same **TRICKs** that affect personal retirement wealth engines can apply to business owners, just in different ways.

Taxes

Business owners are penalized the most when it comes to taxes. Through corporate tax and personal tax, business owners are forced to pad Uncle Sam's pockets. That hurts your business growth.

Risk

Depending on the company or the industry, there can be a lot of risk. As you know, sometimes you can't purchase enough insurance protection for yourself. Errors and Omissions is an example of coverage you can't ever use, because you could never get coverage again. Another issue that can be significant for business owners is the fiduciary risk inherent in many structures necessary just to take care of your employees, such as a 401K. There is also the risk of lawsuits out of the blue over any little thing, or risk from the cost of doing business.

Costs

Also, costs can eat a business owner alive. You might be leaking unquantified money through some unexamined costs, overcharges, or rate discrepancies.

Knowledge Gaps

Often business owners stay in a bad place because they don't know there is more they can do. They are working with generalists; because of the generalists' knowledge gaps, they are poorly equipped to set up an advantageous business plan.

As with individual planning, we help business owners identify the friction in their wealth engine. Then we work with several different specialists to reduce friction and keep your business wealth engine running smoothly, creating the life, business, and DREAM Retirement you want.

BUSINESS OWNER CASE STUDIES

Dr. Milling – Tax reduction and retirement income

Dr. Milling had a very successful ophthalmology practice. When he came to visit us, his son had just committed to joining him in the business. Our initial chat revolved around taxes. Like most folks, he didn't mind paying taxes, but he wished he could pay less.

We went over some preliminary numbers with him, and by following a certain plan, it looked like he could save $60,000 or more per year in taxes. Dr. Milling liked this idea and told me to run the hard numbers. When we sent Dr. Milling all his numbers, his estimated savings was $70,000. His guaranteed annual savings from the tax benefit was $60,000. Needless to say, he was excited about that!

Additionally, the tax plan gave him a way to put away the money for retirement at a tax-preferred basis. This plan was just for him; he did not have to offer it to his employees. And the ultimate benefit is that it will be tax-free when he retires. He has tax advantages both now and at retirement.

The Landers – Tax strategies

Tom and Dianna put a lot of time, money, and resources into their own ophthalmology practice as well; they have been quite successful. However, they always felt that they had a lazy, non-contributing business partner—the IRS. It seemed that the harder they worked and the more they made, the more their unwanted partner would take!

Tom had talked to his CPA and financial advisors. They all told him they were doing everything possible to minimize taxes. But both Tom and Dianne had heard stories from colleagues that told them they were missing something. After one of our events, they came to us to find out what others knew that they didn't. What strategies were available beyond contributing to retirement plans and buying new equipment?

We went to work and identified other strategies to help the Landers save on taxes and apply the funds to their own business. A full tax review with our tax attorney revealed about 12 viable strategies, and Tom and Dianne went from a 39% effective tax rate to a 13% effective tax rate. That was over $70,000 per year in tax savings! They were ecstatic.

As a result of applying these strategies, the Landers were able to both increase their retirement savings and expand their practice. Now they feel they will be able to retire perhaps five years earlier than they had originally planned. That means more freedom to travel and spend time with family, which was why they went into business for themselves in the first place. Now they have greater control over their business and have limited the reach of their lazy, grasping partner. Tom and Dianne have new excitement and anticipation of being able to live their DREAM Retirement—even sooner than they had hoped.

The Parkers - 401K Risk

The Parkers recently came in to talk with us. They are business owners who have a 401K for their employees. They had hired someone to set it up for them and assumed that everything was taken care of. However, as we systematically considered different aspects of their business, they realized that they were carrying 100% of the fiduciary risk for all the plan investments. They didn't even know they were carrying that risk! They thought they had handed it off to the advisor. Intending to do the right thing and benefit their employees with this 401K, the Parkers ended up with a huge liability themselves.

Good news: they did not have to carry this risk. Our full plan review found that their risk could be easily transferred to an outside fiduciary, creating additional benefits for them and their employees while lowering costs also.

"This is a great example of the simple but true saying, 'You don't know what you don't know,'" said Mr. Parker. "We had thought we were doing everything right, but getting a second opinion, a review of our plan, was one of the best things we have ever done."

11. The Color of Money

"We want the blue team to win—right, mom?" Michelle's son Asa often asks this question in the gym or at the field. Blue is the color of the Pointers, our high school team.

We associate many things with colors: the teams we cheer for, traffic signs, types of trucks. As for Asa, his favorite color is red because that is the color of fire trucks! Since we naturally identify things by color, we decided to color money too.

YELLOW MONEY

First, Yellow Money is simply cash reserves or highly liquid assets. You'd probably consider it to be your emergency money, and we advise everyone to put money away in an emergency fund. The principal is not at risk in Yellow Money, but on the downside, growth is next to nothing. So, having too much of your portfolio in Yellow Money can also cause you to take on another risk, that is, inflation. Loss of purchasing power over time will decrease the amount you can buy with the same dollar figure.

Green Money

Green Money is protected growth assets. These offer potentially moderate returns, are tax-deferred or tax-free, and offer partial withdrawals. The principal is protected, and previous year's gains are retained as interest. The annual returns on these assets vary greatly, from 0% to as high as 16%. These assets are designed to be the middle ground between Yellow and Red Money. Generally, Green Money assets offer only partial withdrawals without a penalty for the contract period, which could be anywhere from 2 to 20 years (10 years is the average).

In the investing world, you'll hear people use the term "Fixed Income Asset." This is most widely used when Wall Street talks about bonds. When you buy a bond, your money will be given back to you after it matures. The one problem is that there are no guarantees that it will! Green Money products are bond alternatives, and most follow these three rules.

- Protect principal
- Retain gains
- Guarantee income (when or if you need it)

Green Money is one of the best kept secrets in the financial world.

RED MONEY

Finally, Red Money assets represent risk. Red Money is working money that can lose value. Securities such as stocks, bonds, mutual funds, ETFs, variable annuities, options, REITs, and the like make up these monies. While investors usually see higher gains over time, at the same time these assets can lose significantly in a year—sometimes 30% or more. Your principal is not protected from market fluctuations. Every loss must be recovered 100%, and then growth begins on top of that.

As you approach retirement, your capacity for Red Money risk may decrease—understandably so. However, even in your DREAM Retirement, it may be important to keep some Red Money. You can still avoid significant Red Money losses by following the three M's when investing in Red Money: Measure, Manage and Monitor.

First, Measure the amount of risk you're comfortable with and make sure your investments mirror that level. Then, use Managers and management styles that fit your personal risk level. Then, Monitor their performance. Be sure that the risk you're holding doesn't exceed your comfort level, and reallocate your assets if they do. You can do this management yourself if you like, but you can also take advantage of the services of those who manage and monitor the way you yourself would. This is why you pay your account managers and other financial professionals—so you can enjoy your retirement with peace of mind that it's being handled well!

WHY YOU DIDN'T KNOW THIS

Here is the reason your advisor or manager hasn't told you about all these options: It takes a different license for advisors to offer each of these colors of money. Also, advisors are paid differently on each type of money. Many advisors can't utilize all types of money because of the license of the company they work for. Or they won't offer all types because they prefer being paid in a certain way.

Only an independent advisor, not bound to only one tool- and product-limiting company or brokerage house, will be able to offer both Green and Red Money. Your best-case retirement income scenario is probably some arrangement of both colors; finding an advisor who understands and can access both types is in your best interests.

12. The Cost of Waiting

What is the cost of waiting to paint your DREAM Retirement picture, overhauling your wealth engine, creating your retirement blueprint and implementing the changes? There are a few different ways you can calculate cost.

Wealth and retirement

It's easy to put it off. If your income is fine right now, if you're comfortable with your advisor and what he's telling you, it's easy not to take a close look at what you have.

Remember Ben, who had too much risk in his portfolio in 2008? He lost half his savings and had to work ten more years than he had originally planned. Because he had too much risk that he could have done something about long ago. He might not have lost half his portfolio had he acted earlier, and he might have been able to retire on secure income through 2008.

But suppose you do discover some serious leakage in your wealth engine. When you run the numbers with different tools and different investments and different risk, you might be able to make drastic changes to your retirement income. Imagine discovering this ten or twenty years after you could have made these changes. Imagine the different retirement you could be living with 50% or 100% more income. Think of what you could have done with that money. Think of what you could have left your heirs and the impact you could have had on the charities you believe in.

Benefits

The numbers we run right now might look great. You might say, "I'm good for now; let me come back later and take care of this." However, the numbers will likely not run the same way in a year.

Recently we worked with Terry and Margie. A few years ago, they had some money sitting aside that they thought they could put toward long-term care. This would be a win-win situation: even if they never needed care, the death benefit of the policy (substantially more than the premiums they paid) would go tax-free to a beneficiary. However, they procrastinated. And when they came to us again two years later, they were shocked to find that the long-term care benefits and death benefits were much less than when they first looked two years ago.

There were some reasons for that. One was changes in the economy—low interest rates in this case. Secondly, they were two years older. That always impacts the way the actuaries run the math. Being older makes a big difference with the potential benefit size. Thirdly, in that two years, Margie had suffered a serious medical issue which substantially impacted the benefit.

They could have been so much further ahead if they had acted earlier. Now they were down thousands, simply because they waited. Changes in the economy, the time, or your health can affect your bottom line.

Business advantages

Sometimes waiting could cost you business growth. Did you know that you can implement tax savings plans that will enable you to take advantage of tax credits, put money into your own pocket, and plow money back into the business? Imagine an average difference of $60,000 savings per year.

Now imagine having done this years ago.

Security and control

Finally, the cost of waiting may be catastrophic. You may never get a chance to fix what you failed to do. No one gets a notice that reads, "You're going to have a stroke in two weeks—so get ready." Procrastination is probably the greatest danger to your successful retirement plan. It is possible to procrastinate to the point that planning becomes all but impossible.

What if you have a stroke without a living will or a durable power of attorney in place? Do you know who will make your decisions for you? Will they make the decisions you want to be made?

Suppose you talked about long-term care coverage but never did anything about it. Now you have a car accident that leaves you with disabilities and serious ongoing-care needs. All those expenses are going to come straight from your investments and savings. How long will you and your spouse be able to live on the remainder?

Would you wish this stress upon anyone you love if you could do something now to prevent it?

Sometime we can put an exact dollar amount on the cost of waiting. Sometimes we can't. But the point is, the sooner you take a good hard look and fine-tune the engine, the more likely you are to secure your wealth and growth in a positive direction. The more regularly you review your plan and keep checking for friction, the less likely you are to suffer loss.

13. Are We a Good Fit?

We were asked once how someone could know if it was going to work out when meeting with a financial advisor. After giving it some thought, here's what we know: there must be a good fit for long term success in any relationship. We reviewed all our most enduring relationships with clients and business partners alike and have identified seven key characteristics that exist in all of them.

First, the people in our strongest relationships are people who **live by their values**. Honesty, integrity, and hard work—to name just a few—are the foundational values of everything they do. They do not sacrifice their values for results. The end never justifies the means.

They **know the value of a dollar**. They have worked hard to earn, save and accumulate their money. Mr. Woodley, a Wisconsin business owner, said it best: "Every dollar I have is valuable to me. It came by the sweat of my brow. I risked everything I own to start this business and keep it running. I don't want to pay one more dollar than I am required."

Third, they **believe wealth is more than money**. They understand that true wealth has many dimensions, including personal, spiritual, social, human, and intellectual capital. They believe all forms of wealth are worth preserving. "Relationships are more important than my money," confided Mrs. Hampton, a small business owner. "Of course, I want to have enough to secure my lifestyle now and in retirement, but more than that, I want to positively impact my family, my employees and my community."

They are **open to new ideas**. They know there is no monopoly on good ideas and no corner on creativity. Therefore, they approach new ideas with an open mind. If they are successful, they have a reasonable plan and good advisors, yet they open to new ideas outside their realm of knowledge or sphere of influence that could take them to the next level. Many attribute that quality alone to their success.

They are people who can **make decisions and not look back**. They have the buck stops here mentality. They understand that not making a decision is indeed a decision. "I didn't get where I am by wasting my time or someone else's," said Martina Bryson, retired teacher and principal. "If I have questions, I'll ask them and make up my mind. I'll pick up the phone and call the people I'm working with and make it happen." They ask their honest questions, but they don't stew and second-guess without investigating. And once they've decided, they act.

Sixth, **they know what they do well**, and by implication, **they know what they don't do well**. "I tried the do-it-yourself route with my money. What a disaster!" shared Mr. Wilson, a recently retired businessman. "I know enough to be dangerous. Besides, I can make more money with my time than it costs to delegate."

Last, **they care about quality**. John Ruskin said, "There is hardly anything in the world that some man cannot make a little worse and sell a little cheaper, and the people who consider only price are this man's lawful prey." The people we most like doing business with hire, respect and reward talented specialists ... and desire win-win relationships with the people they enjoy.

These seven key characteristics have been the foundation for every one of our enduring relationships. We look for these characteristics to be evident in everyone we work with: team members, partners, business owners, retired or retiring professionals, and women on their own.

You have worked hard to build your wealth—and you surely know any plan's success depends significantly on the relationships built between major players. Look for these relationship indicators in your own business dealings before making a contractual commitment.

14. A Special Offer for Our Readers

Two of Michelle's sisters recently took a trip around the world. Over three months they visited 15 countries, experienced incredible cultures, and turned many of their dreams into realities.

How did this trip come to be? It started with a dream. Michelle's sister Kim saw a picture of one of her friends riding an elephant through Cambodian jungle. Kim dreamed about doing that too! So she talked to Michelle's other sister Becky, who joined in her dream.

But their dreams did not stop there. They wanted to see the world! Together, they discussed all the places they wanted to visit.

After a few conversations Kim was ready to pack her bags and jump on an airplane. But as we all know, a globetrotting trip is not quite that easy. A person must plan before departing. Even though Kim knew what she wanted to do, she had no idea how. Planning stresses her out—she becomes overwhelmed, freezes, and stays paralyzed. Thankfully, Kim had Becky.

Becky is a planner. Organized to a fault, she planned the entire trip—from hotels to activities to sights to finances. If not for Becky, Kim never would have gone on her dream trip.

Kim and Becky's trip is much like retirement. Most of us have a retirement dream—a list of sought-after destinations and experiences. But we have no idea how to make it happen. Instead of planning, we procrastinate and avoid and ignore. Oh, and hope for the best.

You need a Becky. You need someone who will listen to your dream, then lay out a plan to turn that dream into reality. Let us be your Becky! Our DREAM retirement process walks you through the essential steps to a dream retirement.

Almost everyone desires retirement peace of mind. People want to know their risk level, their monthly income, and their income sources. Your first step toward retirement peace of mind is telling us your dream. Come check out some of our successful past blueprints. Allow us to create a blueprint for you—a plan enabling you to live your DREAM retirement, just as Becky let Kim go on the trip of her dreams. Without Becky, Kim never would have experienced the trip of a lifetime. We want to see you experience the retirement of a lifetime.

Give yourself financial peace of mind and security. Make your DREAM retirement a reality.

Let us be your Becky.

Books are wonderful tools that can help us gain knowledge. Yet, knowledge alone will never change anything...your relationships, your golf game, your health, or your wealth. Change requires *action*.

People often ask what action they should take. Our answer is always the same and simple: Have a conversation with a specialist.

And do it *now*!

Albert Einstein was once asked what man's greatest invention was. Interestingly, he didn't name off any of his inventions or others' inventions. He reportedly said, "Compound interest."

Compound interest has an exponential impact over time, for either good or bad. Mistakes compound as well as successes. You need to act now because compound mistakes will cost you more as time goes on.

As we mentioned, we are on a mission to change the industry—one reader, one retiree, and one business owner at a time. That's why we wrote this book. And that's we are offering our readers the opportunity to have a complimentary Opportunities Conversation with us.

This is an opportunity for you to ask questions about what you read in this book and questions you may have about your personal situation. All information shared with us will be treated with the utmost care and respect to personal privacy.

You will be welcomed at our office and treated to a refreshing beverage and freshly baked cookies as we talk together. You will discover what opportunities exists for you and your family, as well as potential obstacles that could keep you from your DREAM retirement. Most importantly, you will leave knowing what action to take next.

To schedule your complimentary Opportunities Conversation, call 608-987-1511 or email us at fullcircle@bertramfinancial.com.

15. A Personal Note

Now you know the story and the process.

We've endeavored to give you hope for your retirement and restore your confidence that you can live your DREAM Retirement and leave a lasting legacy. You can see the world, cherish your family, and educate the next generation about what is important to you.

If you reading this book and planning your DREAM Retirement (or living it), you are among the wealthiest 1% of the world. Many people will never know what retirement is. They will work until they are too sick to work and then their life ends. They are worried about the next meal. They would never even dream of taking a trip, relaxing on a beach, or just watching their grandkids play ball.

We live in the land of opportunity, freedom and wealth. Therefore, we believe the words of Jesus apply to all of us when He said, "Much is required from those to whom much is given, and much more is required from those to whom much more is given" (Luke 12:48, New Living Translation).

We believe we will all one day stand before God and there will be a few questions He asks us. The first will determine our entrance into Heaven: "Is your name in the Book of Life?" (Did you put your trust in Jesus? Is He your Savior?) The question isn't "Do you believe in any old god?"; rather, it's "Do you personally believe in Me?"

Consider the parable of the rich man and Lazarus.

> Jesus said, "There was a certain rich man who was splendidly clothed in purple and fine linen and who lived each day in luxury. At his gate lay a poor man named Lazarus who was covered with sores. As Lazarus lay there longing for scraps from the rich man's table, the dogs would come and lick his open sores.
>
> Finally, the poor man died and was carried by the angels to sit beside Abraham at the heavenly banquet. The rich man also died and was buried, and he went to the place of the

dead. There, in torment, he saw Abraham in the far distance with Lazarus at his side.

The rich man shouted, 'Father Abraham, have some pity! Send Lazarus over here to dip the tip of his finger in water and cool my tongue. I am in anguish in these flames.'

But Abraham said to him, 'Son, remember that during your lifetime you had everything you wanted, and Lazarus had nothing. So now he is here being comforted, and you are in anguish. And besides, there is a great chasm separating us. No one can cross over to you from here, and no one can cross over to us from there.'

Then the rich man said, 'Please, Father Abraham, at least send him to my father's home. For I have five brothers, and I want him to warn them so they don't end up in this place of torment.'

But Abraham said, 'Moses and the prophets have warned them. Your brothers can read what they wrote.'

The rich man replied, 'No, Father Abraham! But if someone is sent to them from the dead, then they will repent of their sins and turn to God.'

But Abraham said, 'If they won't listen to Moses and the prophets, they won't be persuaded even if someone rises from the dead.'"

– Luke 16:19-31

So we challenge you—to know you can answer the first question, "Yes." Someday it won't matter what kind of retirement you lived or how much you saved in taxes. What will matter is if you know Jesus. Take the warning of the rich man and turn to God.

Second, we challenge you to live as a good steward of all that God has given you—time, talents and wealth. Assuming that you answer the above query with a "Yes," the next question will be "What did you do with what I gave you?" In Matthew 25, Jesus tells a story about separating people during the final judgment.

But when the Son of Man comes in his glory, and all the angels with him, then he will sit upon his glorious throne. All the nations will be gathered in his presence, and he will separate the people as a shepherd separates the sheep from the goats. He will place the sheep at his right hand and the goats at his left.

Then the King will say to those on his right, "Come, you who are blessed by my Father, inherit the Kingdom prepared for you from the creation of the world. For I was hungry, and you fed me. I was thirsty, and you gave me a drink. I was a stranger, and you invited me into your home. I was naked, and you gave me clothing. I was sick, and you cared for me. I was in prison, and you visited me."

Then these righteous ones will reply, "Lord, when did we ever see you hungry and feed you? Or thirsty and give you something to drink? Or a stranger and show you hospitality? Or naked and give you clothing? When did we ever see you sick or in prison and visit you?"

And the King will say, "I tell you the truth, when you did it to one of the least of these my brothers and sisters, you were doing it to me!"

Then the King will turn to those on the left and say, "Away with you, you cursed ones, into the eternal fire prepared for the devil and his demons. For I was hungry, and you didn't feed me. I was thirsty, and you didn't give me a drink. I was a stranger, and you didn't invite me into your home. I was naked, and you didn't give me clothing. I was sick and in prison, and you didn't visit me."

Then they will reply, "Lord, when did we ever see you hungry or thirsty or a stranger or naked or sick or in prison, and not help you?"

And he will answer, "I tell you the truth, when you refused to help the least of these my brothers and sisters, you were refusing to help me."

And they will go away into eternal punishment, but the righteous will go into eternal life.

– Mathew 25:31-46

Not everyone is called to do the same kind of helping as everyone else. There are numberless places to help, from your local community programs or someone sleeping on your streets, to orphanages and micro-loan programs. You can go and give your time, energy, and emotional and spiritual support. You can support these programs and those who do go with your finances and wisdom and prayers.

Serve others. Teach your children and grandchildren. Make an impact in this world. Be like the Good Samaritan: see the hurting, have compassion, stop and help. Live in such a way that you will one day hear Jesus say:

> "Well done, my good and faithful servant. You have been faithful in handling this small amount, so now I will give you many more responsibilities. Let's celebrate together!"
>
> – Matthew 25:23

About Bev and Michelle

Beverly Bertram is a well-known financial educator, speaker and retirement income specialist. Bev has developed a specialty in teaching retirees and those about to retire how to protect their principal and ensure that their money lasts throughout their lifetimes. She has counseled thousands of pre-retirees and retirees how to increase their income, reduce income taxes, avoid taxes on Social Security, avoid estate taxes and protect their estate values.

Bev founded Bertram Financial and has gained over 30 years of real-life experience in financial and estate planning. She is an Investment Advisor Representative, which required her to complete an extensive course of study and pass a rigorous exam proving her comprehensive knowledge in investment issues and personal financial issues.

Bev lives with her husband, Mike, on a small farmette in Mineral Point, Wisconsin, where they have raised nine children. They had four biological daughters and then were blessed to adopt four more daughters and one son. Bev's hobby, when she is not teaching individuals how to obtain more wealth, is spending time with her kids and grandkids, or enjoying the great outdoors, either on foot or horseback.

*****

Michelle Bertram is a well-known financial educator, speaker, author and wealth planner. Like Bev, Michelle is an Investment Advisor Representative. She shares her financial wisdom as a regular guest on radio, including WEKZ-FM. Michelle is a top-rated presenter at universities such as the University of Wisconsin-Platteville. She shows retirees and pre-retirees how to avoid the biggest retirement pitfalls. As a financial educator, she has instructed many groups of pre-retirees, including employees of John Deere, Land's End, Wisconsin State, and the federal government.

Michelle has an Associate's degree in psychology from Ashworth College. She has used her knowledge not only to benefit retirees and pre-retirees, but also to give back to the community through her work with the non-profit organization Operation Go, which she founded. Operation Go focuses on working with local youth and supporting orphanages in Haiti. Very recently, Michelle was honored for this work with an Honorable Mention from Invest in Others, which recognizes and enhances the charitable work of financial advisors nationally.

Michelle lives with her two adopted sons Asa and Asher in Mineral Point, Wisconsin. When Michelle is not changing the world, her hobbies include spending time with her boys and enjoying sporting events. They love to cheer on the local Pointers and the Wisconsin Badgers, as well as professional teams.

Acknowledgements

We are grateful to all who have enriched our understanding of retirement planning.

The colors of money concept originated in Dave Vicks's book *Bat-Socks, Vegas & Conservative Investing*.

Scott Keffer's coaching programs helped us clarify our process. Some content, pictures, and the idea of wealth engine friction came from him

Creating Your DREAM Retirement:
How to Live Your DREAM and Leave a Legacy

Bev and Michelle Bertram
229 High St., Mineral Point, WI 53565

FullCircle@BertramFinancial.com
BertramFinancial.com

ISBN-13: 978-1-946203-01-4
ISBN-10: 1-946203-01-7

Expert Press

www.ExpertPress.net

www.ingramcontent.com/pod-product-compliance
Lightning Source LLC
Chambersburg PA
CBHW050120210326
41519CB00015BA/4043